At the End of the Self-help Rope

Also by New Academia Publishing

MASS FOR NANKING'S 1937, by Wing-chi Chan
THE HOUR OF THE POEM POEM: Poems on Writing, by David Bristol
THE WHITE SPIDER IN MY HAND: Poems, by Sonja James
THE ALTAR OF INNOCENCE: Poems, by Ann Bracken
THE MAN WHO GOT AWAY: Poems, by Grace Cavalieri
IN BLACK BEAR COUNTRY, by Maureen Waters
ALWAYS THE TRAINS: Poems, by Judy Neri

Read an excerpt at **www.newacademia.com**

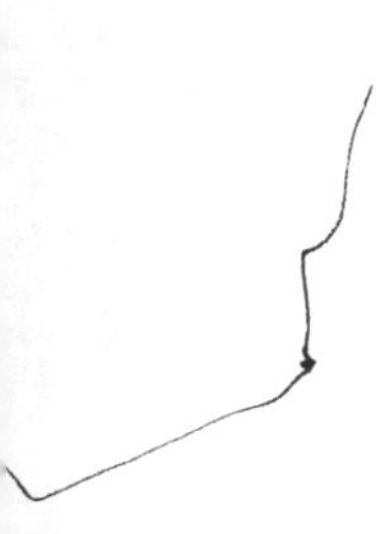

At the End of the Self-help Rope

Poems by Ed Zahniser

Washington, DC

New Academia Publishing 2016

Printed in the United States of America

Library of Congress Control Number: 2015958369
ISBN 978-0-9966484-4-8 paperback (alk. paper)

An imprint of New Academia Publishing

New Academia Publishing
4401-A Connecticut Ave. #236
Washington, DC 20008
info@newacademia.com - www.newacademia.com

For Chris, Justin, Rachel, Jason, Alex, Eric, Katie, Karen, Bob, Esther, Duncan, Matt, and Ann and in grateful memory of Alice and Howard Zahniser, Helen Zahniser Snyder and Lee Snyder, Grace and Paul Oehser, Fred Ethan Fischer, and Greg Lloyd.

Special thanks go to William R. Howard, artist-collaborators Heather Watson and Tom Taylor, John Ellsworth, and Grace Cavalieri, the farrier who shoes us barefoot poets.

Contents

Preface

These poems emerged from Jungian-oriented therapy, group work, a community of faith, and listening to decades of sermons that exhibit life-long learning. The poems owe their form to the late John Berryman and their diction to Berryman, Gerard Manley Hopkins, Olena Kalytiak Davis, and others. They are nourished by long enthusiasm for outspoken ancient poet iconoclasts: China's Hanshan, Persia's Rumi, and India's Kabir, Mira, and Dhurjati. But no one among the above should be held responsible for these poems. May we all make beautiful mistakes and play in earnest — as *Homo ludens,* not merely *sapiens* — to the last line of our last stanza.

Acknowledgements

The Rolling Coulter: Inventory at the Edge, Genealogy of Denial, Prayer for a Hope to Share, Wholly Ghosted, While Angels Weep, Dredging Sleep for Permission to Weep, and Today Admit, Tomorrow Confess.

ART:MAG: Cutting Our Losses
Southern Poetry Review: Taking Stock of Feelings, reprinted in the 50-year anthology
Bradford Poetry Quarterly (U.K.): Soul on Hold (as Homage to Rumi)
Impetus: Male III: In Private Session
Public Hanging!: Dead Reckoning
WPFW-FM Anthology: Sharing Our Stories, and Family Gathering
Antietam Review: Confessing the Body
Showcase XIII: Homage to the Gecko Lizard
Ancient Paths: A Stab at Prayer
The Camel Saloon: Risky Business
Metropolitain: Intercessory and Prayer for Prayer

Heartfelt thanks to Grace Cavalieri, Georgia Lee McElhaney, Hope Maxwell Snyder, Annie Dillard, Randall Tremba, Four Seasons Books, Lisa Olney of Shaharazade's Exotic Tea Room, Bookend Poets, Bookish Group, loyal friends from childhood, and family for unstinting support. I am indebted to A. H. Mathias Zahniser and Karen E. Bettacchi for helpful, close readings of these poems.

When the rest of you
Were being children,
I became a monk
To my own listing
imagination.
— *Frank Stanford*

Is there anyone in the audience who has lived in vain?
— *John Berryman*

It is a thin membrane that separates us from chaos.
— *Chet Raymo*

For the good man to realize that it is better to be whole than to be good is to enter in a straight and narrow path compared to which his previous rectitude was flowery license.
— *John Middleton Murray*

Everyone who is born holds dual citizenship, in the kingdom of the well and in the kingdom of the sick. Although we all prefer to use only the good passport, sooner or later each of us is obliged, at least for a spell, to identify ourselves as citizens of that other place.
— *Susan Sontag*

Suddenly this volume is full. I close it and send it back down with the admonition not to try singing these poems. Only if you sit on them will they do you any good.
— *Shih-wu (Stonehouse)*

I
Support Group

Risky Business

Tonight our topic is risk,
mostly how we do not take it—
or them.
There are hazards: You might slip a disk
or spouse or friend, not quite make it
to the last waltz, or choke on phlegm.

God forbid that we might risk abandonment,
of all drear dreads the adult child's basic fear.
It screws all loyalty to pathology.
And faced with intimacy we act queer:
You can't abandon me if you can't get to me.
We make life's high points punishment.

Damn the torpedoes! Full risk ahead.
Some of us in our circle talked out loud.
Others signaled they weren't dead.
When it comes to taking risks, two's a crowd.
I sat and thought: This is what I need to hear.
I also thought: Let me out of here!

Making Amends

We read our book around the circle,
a chapter a week, then talk
not by turns but by compulsion
whose needs we know too well. Its miracle
moves most of us to speech despite how chalk
mounds in our mouths just then.

This week we list exactly everyone we've hurt
and, what is worse, must make there-from amends
for our lifetimes of dirty deeds.
Are you kidding? My accumulated dirt
mounds deep. To probe it hazards the bends
or pushing up noxious weeds.

What veils our spirits slowly rends,
slowly, soothed by tears, gratis,
as is our protocol.
From here on out, make your own amends.
This former fixer's new-won status
is deserter. He's no more AWOL.

Today Admit, Tomorrow Confess

Do not fear this day
whose Sun will rise, then orb the sky and set
—with you or without you.
February seems designed to pave the way
to that horizon you would rather not have met,
but do not fear this day. I do.

Late winter's flu screams nightmares in my head:
feathers flying from an antique pillow,
Vicks VapoRub's heady fumes,
grandmas coming back from the dead,
my baby blanket, teddy bear. But please no
chicken soup fat's yellow algal blooms.

I admit it: I am powerless
over the effects of my addiction,
which are not to admit it and then deny
the sinking feeling. Today admit; tomorrow confess.
Come March, if it will, I may decide
to donate my body to science fiction.

Taking Moral Inventory

Now for a searching and fearless moral inventory:
Fetch pen and paper, quick!
Let's rate ourselves against the Seven Deadly Sins.
We'll storm the Sea of Morality by hunky dory.
—Face it, no one wins.
Still ticks this deathness unto which we're sick.

From sackcloth, stout, a voice of iron—Do I dream
or is this someone dreaming me? Manic wails
this pastor? priest? or prophet? The latter, it would seem.
No one rushes to gird me with gladness
any more than Jesus rushed to proffer Pilate nails.
Destination: the pit, by way of madness.

Spare, balanced, quiet, I bow
to simpler beings.
Let's stake our lives again in what we dream
and dream as big as the Super Bowl.
Lord. Temptress. Therapist—someone: make me whole
and bid me live one moment in the now.

Keep Coming Back, It Works

Across our self-help circle someone bottoms out
—shouldering paroxysms of sobbing punctuated by
apologies for self-pity, confessions of self-doubt,
and sundry inner execrations money cannot buy.
I know her feeling. A slant of numbness in the head
and suicide looks like a week at Club Med.

Someone else's family ostracizes her
"because you go to meetings." She wants to get well,
which wish betrays *their* sickness bred in Hell.
(Fix me a drink and put some menace in my slur.)
What can we tell each other but "Keep it up!"
we scions of our lengthy lines of sick, sick pups.

We do. We empathize. We hug our weird ways out
of it. I find I envy anyone their lowest point,
their nadir of all fears. How lucky, it happens here,
not home at Christmas, putting loved ones out of joint.
My grandmas pegged our angst as faithless doubt,
pulping it with scripture verse and gobs of prayer.

Nurturing Our False Selves

"I love myself," he said, burnishing
the commonplace with flagrant oxymoron.
His eyes betrayed a further twist
to expectancy, as though his inner child
might have transgressed a boundary
elusive as an edge of the Milky Way.

Even in his chair tonight he looked
like Br'er Rabbit locked in Tai Chi
combat with the dreaded Tar Baby.
After the meeting we vent our crosstalk
if only as interior monolog.
Dreamless sleep or sleepless dream,

which would you choose?
History nor fact suffice.
All day an unacknowledged feeling
sacked me like a quarterback
running a double reverse solo,
mid-field, mid-life, mid-all and -nothing.

Owning Up and Letting Go

Nonstop tirades of ugly vitriol
—from his coffin in a dream her father
won't shut up but yaks and yaks at her.
He is in fact dying, but why does she bother
not to let him? All her life this utter cur
gnashed his teeth at her soul.

Once a week we make our circle here
to confront dysfunction's needs.
"I'm an adult child of well-meaning parents,"
says someone clutching anger in her fear.
"Let go and let God" is how another vents
the urge to rescue others from their foul misdeeds.

"My name is Ed, and I'm an adult child
of an overly religious family system."
"Hi, Ed!"
Suddenly, my tongue feels like a twist-em.
It's December—in this life? this year? Weather mild
except a blizzard rages in my head.

Protocol

Her dog—let's call him Beppo
for anonymity's sake—
cradles like a stuffed toy in her arm
noiseless tonight. In fact, no
one called on him. Did he also ache
to bark but fear that doing so might harm

his image? Well, it's not group protocol
to call on man nor beast.
Our Higher Power moves us
—or we're not moved at all.
Frustration leavens like baker's yeast.
Our urge to rage gets muted to mere fuss.

Some nights I would like to bark
or, better, to howl at the waning moon.
I'd turn this group into Noah's Ark
listing on our last pontoon.
We ache for shore leave, to blow our cool.
Life is too much like Obedience School.

Let Go and Let God

Innocence vanished long ago:
in Virginia once an older woman
tried to teach him things, he says,
"I still don't seem to know."
What happened and what's happening now:
That's the garden we gather to tend

like roses of impossible descent.
Answers sound at first like car doors
slamming down a street you do not know.
Vague threats sharpen knife-dark air.
"Don't talk, don't trust, don't feel."
Childhood litanies ensnare us still.

"Maybe I should start facing puberty,"
he laughs. Such emotions and more
leap to the playing floor like cheerleaders
at halftime: "Go! Go! Let's go let go!"
Turn it over, yes, the pain and agony, but
turn it over how? Turn it over where?

Theater in the Round

Angst, ennui, despair; our weekly circle
mimics the Theater of the Absurd.
We play it in the round and fill
all player-audience roles,
but the orchestra pit sits vacant.
We score improvised scripts

with titters and tears and nothing
more percussive than a blowing nose
except when a fist might pound
to defy at last good childhood manners.
"Manners suck!" one woman prompts, invoking
Emily Post as a dried-up prune.

They say that from God's distance
our worldly hustle-bustle makes
a soothing drone, even our human rancor.
I'm glad for God. I'm also glad for distance.
Give me more from my childhood,
and then play on, you sweet absurdity.

I'm Okay, Aren't I?

"What I've done is never good enough,"
raps the three-way cross-talk in her head.
"I don't tend to look at the good things,
at the good I've done."
Early on she decided she's not okay.
The goal eludes her still.

She leads our group tonight
her first time ever, and leads it well.
No one nods off. We broach
essential shames of never measuring up,
of the politics of self-sabotage,
and "Why can't I be valued just for me?"

We can, of course, and are,
but don't know how to convince ourselves.
In the recesses of my mind it's still
recess. "Teacher, where's the playground?"
Someone quips: "The mind's the second thing
to go." The goal eludes me also still.

What Do You Think About One Night a Week?

At the end of the self-help rope
someone in our circle pours their guts out.
Another yawns
across this chasm of guilts—booze, sex, or dope
—and millionous takes on self-doubt.
Something there is that on us never dawns.

Sow bears evict me from my own fraught dreams.
Hot wafts of dirt-tinged camas-lily breath
pant steamy down my flimsy neck.
She just dined on mule deer! I choke on screams
and cannot run.
The race would seem to be to death.

Islands adrift in a sea
of entropy,
we float as sick as our secrets.
Guts spilled to yawns, our circle rankles.
This won't work, folks. Extend regrets.
The sky can't fall. It's down around our ankles.

Thin Gruel

"Even those of us who stayed at home
were orphans," she says and then
looks blank. Her memory strays
out past the far, frayed end of common sense.
"Do I feel sorry for myself?
No, but for my children."

More blankness clouds her screen
as long interior arguments ensue.
Too much religion, not booze or dope,
haunts her past like weird chips
off what was once a sacred block. Glitches
garble old hymns to stoned lyricism.

"No, but for my children."
Some of us come to these weekly meetings
so *they* won't have to.
Silence amplifies the heater-housing's hum.
Our children's comfort makes thin gruel.
An inner child still may starve.

Thursdays Are Group Night

Wouldn't a legacy be nice?
Pay off the mortgage, car, and
credit cards. You know, take a break
from work, the job, and really hone in
on your navel like laser aircraft
auto-pilot landing gear. Oh boy!

A legacy? Her parents left her instead
dysfunctional feelings: a personal
responsibility for the latest war.
"I can't help it," she says, "I
just know there's something, something
I could have done to have prevented it."

Outside this church basement far stars
Dance to the Doppler effect, seeming
to laugh: "And you think you're so bright?"
Far stars do dance, and we do dream a legacy
of health this time. Contemplate our navels?
Better to howl at the moon.

Losing a Scab

She wears deep pain facially
like Frankenstein's monster's suture.
Her skin goes gray, bones flattened. You'd swear
it's something she hangs onto, not especially
important on the cosmic scale. You can see where
soon she could complete her future.

Our topic is Letting Go. "Like losing a scab,"
someone offers. "It's almost unconscious."
Kerplunk!
A psychic scab but a freaking hunk.
Tell me this itch wears off. Don't mention pus.
"Let go and let God," our motto mottles, drab

beyond description. I stifle mine:
"Let go and let God
then let God go."
Our flaws compete to confuse our kids. As odd
is hyper-religiosity. But what a way to go!
Observe the curve to my spine.

Anger's Inner Rant

A beetle bites a frog, injects its venom,
and waits while organized amphibious innards
rush to mush. Then *whoosh*: Slick sucking
saps said frog to voided skin.
"Anger's inner yammer sucks me dry,"
she caps her cheery anecdote in sum.

Our soft bumbling babble
simulates a burbling brook.
She does resemble her own shell
stuck streamside listless on its rock.
Our group completes her circle
with inner lives expert at making Melba Toast

of the Bread of Life. God, you may frown
but grant us Zwieback or biscotti lest we revert
to toothless gums. Raw anger dull and frozen,
feckless rage. Resentments self-chosen
drip resounding torture on their welling pond. Alert
at least, we founder so as not to drown.

Overdubbed by Parent Tapes

In artful speech rich with dense prose
she denies our humanity, says
"even lovers only follow their nose,"
then, flushed with confused passion, she prays,
expressing not one untoward wish
in flawless King James Version English.

Good God, help us, please, to put
some order to our years and years
of self-help books, of self-reliance
seminars, and gobs of psychotherapy.
Free us from past pain and pull us
screaming from this dreamlike state.

Image our dilemma:
one rock, one hard place, us between.
In semi-darkness seldom-seen
horrors of our own devising lurk. Give them a
hand for having brought us, low, this far.
They're light as feathers. Here comes the tar.

Scrupulous Critiques

Abandonment and self-destruction sought:
"I need a crisis," he says, "or someone
even sicker than I am."
Dusk falls outside these basement windows.
He recounts one blind date
"like being cornered by a Jesus freak."

Let's talk about my problems, okay?
Good, you talk about them.
I can't. Anger frozen since childhood
threatens spring breakup's torrential rampage
through our narrow neighborhood.
Night darkness settles. Basement

windows turn one-way mirrors now.
We meet in this church nursery,
inner children undergoing scrutiny.
"Nevertheless," he concludes, "this is
like 'friends are falling out of trees.'"
How odd, his metaphor of brotherly love.

Coping Mechanisms Wear Out

"Don't argue with me. I know I'm right!"
She was always the clever one,
he tells us. She'd always win.
A sad wind ventilates his gills tonight,
green from something he has done
by way of routine self-destruction.

"Thanks for sharing that," we say, almost
in unison and half by faith, half rote.
"Keep coming back, it works!"
He hovers above his chair, a ghost
on whom a mother might cringe to dote.
Odd, how we render terminal the quirks

of childhood survival ploys.
Family trees bear poisonous fruit
persisting to pretend itself benign.
Denial and mistrust, favorite toys,
left our feelings destitute.
Show me my Higher Power so I can resign.

A Stab at Prayer

Ricocheting resolutions, if each were a new year
I'd be senior to Methuselah
and still as checkered as plaid.
I see the ocean, where's the chart? Old fears
still ply their flat-world way.
Just for today I will not be afraid.

Strange God, do you like me? Good. Then
what do you want me to do
or undo. You name it, faith or deeds.
I'll make that list of faults that's utterly true
and be the second to admit: I have these needs.
What more can I say? Of course, Amen.

But not quite yet. Do help me, Higher Power!
Help me put an order to these years
of reading self-help books.
Before I turn them, pages sour.
I'd meditate but fear the inner dirty looks.
At Heaven's gate do not heed my tears.

Today's Agenda

Drop all denial. Indulge emotions
heretofore unfelt
and pummel figures of authority
until we raise one vast, undifferentiated welt.
Entertain God with streams of blasphemy,
assailing enemies with dreadful puns.

"I will fight no more forever," a chief once said.
"I flat give up!" said someone else:
The battle? The War? Life itself? The ghost?
Pick any battlefield and count our sprawling dead
—or take your pulse.
What do you promise to grieve the most?

I grieve: not unlike sweet music, her downturned face,
its self-contained perfections, like higher math
or the twist of an anthem choosing its awkward path
that straightens toward uncommon grace.
I grieve these flights of my spirit
winging out of sight. I wanted to stay near it.

Taking the Controls

Let me good God, please, tell you how I feel:
Last night our topic was our Higher Power,
but I awoke again this morning flying low.
No matter how I bellow at the radio
silence echoes from the control tower
while the runway rises all too real,

and my landing gear stuck up,
as you doubtless know, in childhood.
How long can I circle so low overhead
like a languid tail wagging its sick pup?
If I can't beat these controls, I'm dead.
You take them. That would be good.

Last night in a dream of an otherwise
friendly field, a long and fat, fierce snake
chased me down and faced me off.
Was that you, co-pilot, in disguise?
We need to talk, one-on-one. What does it take?
Let's talk about my chronic winter cough.

Remembering First Nights

New to our group tonight she asks,
half to us, half to herself, "What
was it someone called me? Yes,
'a mutants magnet.'" She attracts
defective men—like us? A workaholic nut
was her latest. You'd never guess:

He worked his ass off but billed no client
so that, broke, he'd have to toil harder!
Aren't we loonies out there?
Or here? A child could mold no fearsomer giant,
nor mystic image a more muddled martyr.
Mutants—you have to laugh or blankly stare

if you also fill the bill
full as a balloon—
we rage, we scream and screech—
or blimp, hoping to rise above the urge to kill.
My first night I brooded, a dumbstruck buffoon.
Now I prattle on like a campaign speech.

Fronting Sexual Addiction

She takes off her cloak and—*nothing*.
The Invisible Woman
whose smallest pebble tossed into the ocean of
organic life sets more tempest in the offing
than her life's collected dreams misunderstand.
Tonight our topic is love

whose grubby finger probes
dangerously close to the lately dormant heart.
Outrun your grief forever?
You can't; nor stuff it into art.
Grief wears you as the Emperor's new clothes.
This love you cannot sever

like your Siamese twin and not bleed to death
in that desperate act.
Earth thrusts volcanic
magma hardly hotter than passion's breath
as flesh renews a claim to primal fact.
She is entitled to her panic.

Toxic Parents Wearing War Paint!

Her parents hold a lump sum over her
like a skyscraper wrecking ball
every so often
swung into action. Now her daughter
seems to her to live inside stout walls
no good intentions crack.

Some family curse our common legacy.
We come to our weekly circle stunned
like frogs kids slammed against the pond.
The trick's to not deny responsibility
but not persist to eat our parents' share. Shunned
emotionally, we want the white magician's wand

to wave for us its healing touch.
Weekly we circle the wagon trains
bent on collective self-protection.
Sometimes it works like a rubber crutch
or placebo fighting labor pains.
At least now we face the right direction.

Extra Credit for Childhood

His head is a form of no content.
Being accepted and clever
turn out not to be the point of life.
In relationships he can't make a dent.
His stuckness begs too long a lever
for ever prying loose: "Ask my wife

if you can find her."
His father tried to make the world unsafe for pride
and died proud that he'd done it.
In any success something better
could have happened. "Oh yeah? So shove it!"
let's shout from anger long denied.

Criticism was taboo, but the criticism
of criticism ran rampant,
contradictions thick like tar-pits goo.
Who needs mental illness? Schisms
define our equilibrium as erratic cant.
Childhood earned us extra credit in voodoo.

II
Inventory at the Edge

That His Muse Mourn His Losses, Too

She only wanted him to act just like Columbus, see?
To set full expeditionary sail
for unmapped lands across a sea white on the charts.
She'd inked hers full—he had *no* self, and less memory—
so instantaneously in such detail
it scared him stiff. "Am I a figment of her art?"

She sensed his typical predicament:
"to mature, achieve, then be reduced"
bewildered by a past that's unresolved.
Steering by naught but numbness and some stars,
he bumps along collision's course between
desire and regret with sighs for fuel.

Radio silence now: layer on layer
his grief makes onions seem skin deep.
It sections his shattered heart
like geologic faults. To weep
would go volcanic. Better to wail in prayer.
Of all he's met he is apart.

Inventory at the Edge

False starts, lost ambitions, half-sight
and doses of darkness,
inner, outer, all-pervading. We plod
toward Easter down February's tunnel, whose light
end might be resurrection. Confess:
survival looms as metaphor for God.

Ask any nation in its Exodus
dreaming cloud-guides and pillars of fire
while eating wilderness Wonder Bread.
After 40 years who wouldn't fuss
despite the dazed-eyed patriarch whose ire
renders enemies fields of dead,

and whose finger might finger you?
I see things in my own night.
Faint shadows map this wild wall
of sleepless staring, nothing plumb, nothing true.
Winds whip up a constant fright.
Forever shy of the promise we stall.

Genealogy of Denial

Fear of abandonment haunts me:
disease with no cure
and terminal, although death would make no dent.
Sickness hangs in the air, an agent free
to nail my children's children. Lines blur
in our family tree's stunted bonsai monument

to our cult of the dull pruning knife.
Bloodless human sacrifice
makes for a lifelong coup
exacted by denying strife.
Our brand of Christian is Minute Rice
—you can't imagine the cost of dues.

We tithed emotion by careful collusion
then gave up feeling for Lent.
Successful sacrifice—it never went
away or grew back.
We made of faith a cul-de-sac
and drown in its scrupulously hidden ocean.

Cutting Our Losses

Out the window the ghost of Fred the Cat
under low-grown maple branches sat
hunkered down against light rain.
He stared at me pellucidly
through the wet stillness heavy
on my lingering brain.

Sea level rises. The Sun, a dwarf star,
burns slowly out. Strong
across a lake entire a woman swims
determined, as though across her personal bar.
She has lost what she cannot measure and skims
the surface and cannot talk of it.

Who would suspect
that bees have set up housekeeping
inside her? She does but in what limb?
She listens to their wild interior humming.
She puts an ear to here, and here, and there.
Onshore, faint breezes work the wands of greasewood.

Taking Stock of Feelings

Aches my left foot, arch already flat,
flat, too, my former rectitude's flowery license.
I crave support and moist warmth snug as a glove
yet tenuous, like a wide-brimmed hat
lodged against a windstorm's heady violence.
Not to mention love.

Nothing gives but what it gets
used up, worn out, or failing that
contents itself to feed the Universe
while guilt worries its spectrum like a rheostat
—or blows me skyward on jets.
I can't remember when, but I have felt worse.

Hostage monkhood's blindfolded silence has gone.
Damnable thing, suspected, you never hear it
pass like an empathy between captive and captor.
Clangorous birdsong squelches my spirit,
a rabbit frozen before this swooping raptor.
Sweet Christ, I'm flat out. It's only dawn.

Soul on Hold

I've traded in my theism, atheism, and agnosticism.
I'm in a simple state—no mean feat—
where space and time are discrete.
So are, one from the other, either ear,
for which my head evolved as their schism.
I do wish for my way to appear.

The cat is busy rehearsing its next nap.
I don't much want to know the future,
but I do want to watch it unfold.
We dance with separate broomsticks, or run laps.
My body binds my soul by a gossamer suture.
You call it, umpire—dross or gold?

An ocean, formless, dooms a rudderless barge.
Awkward, in this dream, a woman, overlarge,
presents her archetypal tit.
In the first half of life I was not fed, she said,
the living bread.
But now I am it.

Fear of Removing Blind

Birdsong wafts through the cracked window
on the odor of early frost.
Beige and tasting of metal, already
the weighty box of a childhood lost
wakes to haunt me, taunt me
like a violin played with hacksaw bow.

Where is that man in me
you might classify as wild?
As primal, not as savage, possessed of power
for gentleness, love, and peace?
It would have paid to have been a child
—not this imploding meteor shower,

this hopelessly twisted Rubix cube.
Stars go haywire, rock and jounce.
Galaxies vomit their masses whole.
Death energies cannot wait to pounce
on an un-integrated soul.
Can I get this toothpaste back in the tube?

The Shadow on the Menu

It's in the bag! Meaning most of me.
Stuffed, stashed, and long denied,
my shadow lies in the bag I drag behind
me in a blind spot. Maybe, just maybe,
you can see it. Had I more often cried—
and sooner—it might have come to mind.

Weighty, it holds most of my childhood,
its energy, curiosity, aggression, fear,
the anger a parent didn't like,
the stuff that schools misunderstood,
and what teen-aged peers thought queer.
It holds instincts told to take a hike.

Good God, let us breach the bag
not grandly with machete but with tweezers.
In bite-size chunks I need to eat my shadow.
Give me back my inner witch, that lovely hag.
Give back my greed, to stomp my people pleasers.
I want to love so much of me, to love and know.

No More Suicidal Fantasies

Grief so deep his toes curl.
His head at once devolves
into an echo chamber for racked sobbing.
Would he have cried some sooner, born a girl?
No, the real question involves
who or what persists at robbing

his collusive quick
and egging on his would-be dead?
Months or mere weeks ago it seems
there was no self to kill, so sick
he'd grown, retreating to a corner in his head.
Colorless, his dreams

grew colorless, waking or sleeping.
He dreamed them back. A spark in his head
lit accumulated litter on his heart.
Paroxysms of weeping
prove antidotes to promenading with the dead.
Now he will live by fits and starts.

Asking Directions in a Foreign Tongue

A dead man tries to convince himself
of the benefits of coming back to life,
where indeed he may not quite have been
since his childhood got lost. Toys on the shelf
became an inward knife
with most alluring sheen.

Emotionally catatonic on the sea wall
beach-side he sulked in stony terror—
how the careful lid set early on life
might flip, and some Vesuvius erupt
to kill them all,
all but six. Save six to bear his pall.

In life and death we belong to God
—so what's the difference?
I only wish I didn't think I know again.
If these poems shout, don't think it odd.
I've learned long since
how I began them stone deaf to my pain.

Prayer for Prayer

Solitude so perfect it's not lonely:
grant us, merciful God, this sense
just once of satisfying prayer,
each of us your one and only
supplicant. We'll bat across the back fence
dark things difficult to share.

We'll find new words. Nothing off-the-shelf
can quite express this urgent need
simply to confess, unburden, and unbind.
Most prayers turn out like talking to yourself
even with the spirit up to speed
and quiet to mollify the mind.

Accept our words and thoughts as psalms
or even a pitiful candle lamp
that quavers toward the author of desire.
Admit their doubt. Admit my qualms.
I feel like a primate creeping into camp
to worry the embers from your fire.

Private Session

I choked but stuffed it. Plateaus of platitudes
landscaped me dull with unspoken feelings.
Why can't I rage and destroy the City of Gotham?
Turn upside down benign Beatitudes?
I'd feel better after a few good reelings
in typhoon-like anger. I've hit bottom,

but didn't feel the *bump*.
My funk a black hole powerless for attraction.
My cancer (points to head) this condensed lump
like a backpack hoard of choked retraction,
emotive or sensate.
Longevity may have to wait.

I'm exhausted with being flawless because I'm not.
A luscious breast renders me mentally defective
(let's not talk morals but only what's effective).
If that is hell, I volunteer to rot.
A parent decades dead absconded
with the key that locked me in my head.

Dead Reckoning

Our father who art already in heaven
give us this day our daily death
but not a jot or tittle more.
Cycles and numerology are a crashing bore
but I'll admit I cringe for most of any year
divisible by seven

that threatens to zap my world as I know it.
Spilled, the beans, your guts. Loosed, your marbles
and then your midriff buttons *popped*.
Midlife finds me chastened—did I blow it?—
by whatever confuses, unhinges, or garbles.
If this is God, God should be stopped.

Seething anger, abject disappointment, blind violence
—one more emotion from the mail-order catalog?—
grieved, brooding silence.
Dry-docked, my captain keeps a shadow log
that won't condemn dead-reckoned navigation.
On deck a charmer, below he defies imagination.

Sharing Our Stories

He noticed things exactly
so he could twist the facts
to somewhat truth with the clear eye
of a hurricane. Flailing in mystery
he found fits of sleep in random acts
of pointed humor, wry and dry.

The seduction of fled charms
besets the brain and breaks the heart.
A silhouette, a shaken fist,
stuttering lives pinned in death's arms
—You overstate the case, which harms
our cataloging all we've lost, or missed.

Heaps of fragments can't resolve
how insect thoughts steal thunder's voice. Hey!
Some magic now: Jack's stalky beans
and a golden goose for drug of choice.

Language is our only way
and means.

Prayer for a Hope to Share

Forced so long to hope alone
can we find a hope to share
—and unreservedly?
We're out of time for throwing half a bone
each to each. Half to care is not to care
at all. The path looms swervingly,

what with the cross put at our backs.
How odd to hope on a death
with a long, still longed-for promise of return.
Two thousand years following in tracks
as gossamer as, however holy, spirit breath.
All is vapor. Yet I cannot help but yearn

to turn and turn again, to put my face
to that persistent promise.
What fabric lasts without its knowing weaver
to restore these tatters to a former grace
however flawed? I would miss
the curious comfort of the true believer.

III
Midlife with Morning Paper

Grieving the Loss of a Teenage Love

Sleep after no sleep, it is best,
all other succor
being distant and estranged—or playing dead.
Half a Xanax brought him rest.
Maybe if he does enough of them his head
will be as beautiful as Marilyn Monroe's, or

his dreams bat like her slugger Joe DiMaggio
—and his plays be hits like Arthur Miller's.
After the fall comes, drama or no, winter.
Is he ready? No,
not his bronchi, which can be killers,
nor for this icicle driving like a splinter

through his arrhythmic heart?
Do not, good God, let it drop
from this year's choked-up eaves.
Our losses reap their bumper crop.
Why can't we disappear in art
like children in a pile of autumn leaves?

Holy Fire

He remembers the lifeguard,
a then-young woman many, many
summers now long gone, long before
his major role in life (swallows hard)
was *not*—not to drop any
of umpteen balls he juggles or

put another way, to curb
each impulse to upset the balance
carefully kept by constant motion
like a gyroscope. To disturb
one detail, one iota now would chance
to breach confining comfort, a notion

grown too horrid to acknowledge.
Nevertheless, he remembers her now
like an old flame flickering to scorch
the wraps kept on such dreams since college.
Alert yet languid, she—he remembers how
she fused his passions like a welding torch.

Wholly Ghosted

Roles reversed in freak-show middle life
now he distorts the mirrors, absent carnivals of choice.
Thins, the brain, and thickens, the bod.
Desperate and reversed, prayers scream at God
who remains with infinite silence rife.
Once in that herbal haze, he heard a voice

within: "Serve the Lord. Serve the Lord."
Genetic memory? Perverted shaman in the weed?
He stands agnostic now of after-the-fact analysis.
What to do: trade his Chevy for a Ford?
Hug the Dow Jones so hard it bleeds?
He's opting for metaphysical paralysis.

A voice absent a body: When it sounded for
you, what then? Did you dance in the temple
naked like King David? Say "Here am I, Lord. Your
servant is listening," with young Samuel?
Our hold on sanity ices, thinner than our skin,
too thin to tolerate another voice within.

Living for Others Leaves Few Memories

Sidetracked in the world of sleep and dream
he snuffles along in armadillo consciousness
with old survival ploys for armor plates.
In his father's house no mansion, a self-less scream
suppressed, and a taboo on compliments.
He slumps to contemplate

just how that taut taboo
—what were this lost child's feelings?—
got him so he might believe or feel
himself anything for this moment that might do
to make him soar—or bob along the ceiling—
for having pleased a father who affixed said seal

upon affection with a brittle wax.
"I call this 'mind over Matt,'"
his brother said of the agonies that ensued.
Success seems to argue so-called facts
like ginger ale gone flat, as flat
as this ghost we have not never wooed.

Midlife with Morning Paper

Chaos and confusion or
dysfunction and disorder?
What's happening here?
We think we know. Okay, we don't know.
Things are passing strange or else unclear.
Brains drift high with snow.

Freud put it best:
"Emma, what's for breakfast?"
Item: the classical music host just failed
by a month to make it to retirement (August,
he had planned). A tightness in the chest,
and God was that taxi driver he'd never hailed

in the driving downtown rain
when, as Ogden Nash once said,
taxis are rarer than the whooping crane.
Cranes make their comeback now
but not from the individual dead.
We must learn *how*.

facing death

Intercessory

An old, old friend writes from Oregon
his litany of woes.
Midlife and parenting combine
to baffle him: "Where has life gone?"
and "Are these wrenching throes
the deal from here on out?" We whine

only less coherently
and count the fleeting days. December
digs like an ice-pick at the heart.
Where even to start?

What is it safe to remember?
Fear fosters brevity.

The Prayers of the Community will rise
this Sunday morning all across our town.
We rise in time to sit beneath them,
breath pushing angst toward wintry skies.
Henny Penny was right. God, don't be dim
in Oregon this day. Do smooth that frown.

Like a Rolling Stone

"Happy Birthday! How does it feel,"
an old friend writes, "to be closer to fifty
than to forty?" How to handle that
and not feel like a fifth wheel
reinvented flat,
thumping down the highway. How nifty.

Certifiable in retirement, his dad
couched out, the friend recounts, and hit the bottle
"alcoholic by anyone's definition."
But even before, "the pathology was as bad.
I got the full load." And the realization
how your inner child can choke at half-throttle.

Now his own stomach rolls, he says, too frail
for drink—as once it was for Boy Scout cooking.
Other obsessions now must do.
How does it feel? I've trimmed the sail.
I own no grave plot yet but am looking.
So few things seem new.

While Angels Weep

Sanctus by Benoit: The organ prelude
further swells this summer-swollen air
the ceiling fans strain to separate.
Robe-less the minister allows as how
"Angels weep at how we strut on Earth"
and that "Our God rules not

with an iron fist but with such love"
and "We are made in that image" so
"Are not we also loaded with such power?"
A good question, but the service seems
to end absent an answer.
We rise slowly from humid pews,

unconvincing as gods and goddesses.
Stiff knees anticipate
our benediction as a good word
hopes to hold us one more week
while angels weep, hopes to bolster us
another week while angels weep.

Prayer, after Long Silence

Deep into that double life
—this angel/animal race—
he merely flirted with coherence.
Light the past!
No, make more light the present
with its vast delicious burdens

he still carries here. Make them open
out onto the rich and passing strange,
peerless in our neighbor's story.
Formless chat, spent skill,
and worst this wasted faith.
Let him give up all, becoming rich.

Your house holds firm; we decay.
Discontinuous amidst mad-lyric mode,
good God let us most perplex
those we most enchant
until these fetters jail the mind no more,
and you alone are left to mind our store.

Confessing the Body

Tantum ergo; "Therefore, we,
before Him bending, this
great sacrament revere."
My body and her blood not dis-
continuous. The latter blots all fear
as stain and seal of immortality.

What better wine but our own fluids?
And for bread? Our wedded lust
all other hungers must
at last postpone;
parts of us erect, like stones of Druids
who watch nor setting now nor rising sun alone.

Tell Edmund Waller this:
intrusions of magnificence, her breasts
here heavy on me lie
bulwarks against our passage west
—our Mother Lode, longevity—
whose flesh of sainthood I do dearly kiss.

Ritual to Un-stuff His Shadow

Yin and Yang engulf him consciously at last.
Still he needs damned well a black crow ally
—or hawk that reeks of rodent breath.
Positive dark intrudes but not fast
enough to suit. Too long he sat idly by,
collusive accomplice to his own slow death.

Will he plunk pallid gray in a wheelchair
—pray not soon—
still lusting after victim women
with brain-dead stare
like the feeling-defective baboon
he had become? So be it and Amen.

The heart has reasons reason does not know,
didn't Pascal say?
Breasts, lovely, nurturant
—how I early missed you.
And in my worn soul's darkest night
I want the more to kiss you,
kiss you long and long and slowly slow.

Reincarnation Reconsidered

Not holy but, worse, half terror,
dodging judgments like grapefruit-sized hail.
The brown meadow lies beaten flat by winter.
No margin but error.
Reduce a life to a splinter
but do not jam it up its own black fingernail.

Stale odors of musky death-wish vie with
denial's stony silence and penetrating smells
of disinfectant poised to swab this parting mess.
Sick to death of sickness,
health recedes into a radio-wave myth
broadcast in elevators to mask these hells

of aggressive collusion.
Pass the glass of hemlock
please, life's losses replete.
Why take further stock?
He implodes on lone confusion.
Birth looks like nothing to repeat.

Family Gathering

At our mother's 70th, someone asked
his brother how it felt, his turning 50?
"You can't escape the fact," he said
"a door has closed behind you,"
then swallowed visibly.
We adjusted our suits or dresses

for the coming photo session
complete with nine grandchildren.
Christopher Columbus hit 50
in prison, shackled and manacled
for perturbing his royal sponsors.
By then he knew he'd not set foot

on North America's mainland.
I want to turn 70 if only
for longevity's sake. Then I, too,
will panic like a spent bull elk
plagued by lungworms during the rut
in the heart of grizzly country.

Dredging Sleep for Permission to Weep

Lost in morning's half-sleep:
London in a dream, but Berry's southern home
(He's never seen). Forgot his transit pass!
The woman with half a face like a gnome
fails to teach him how to weep.
No tears, but how his mouth does foam.

A conflict between two poets, one, Irish,
but dreamed as Jewish here, who
having cut off his hand cannot respond
when questioned why. A death-wish?
Unresolved religious goo?
The other bard wields house rules like a wand.

He wakes tired, more racked with care
than when he went to bed at ten.
Again tonight, again, good God, why?
Verbal storms, half-terror: There,
you're doing it again!
Quit sticking your finger in his eye.

The Second Definition of Every Word Is Loss

Cook these sedimental dreams
to igneous bedrock faith.
Death rains from the inland sea overhead
its fossil-bent wrack of calcified screams.
The shadow of his former waif
lugs losses to the verge of dread.

Renew a simple urge to turn,
face-to, to heaven's cauterizing fire
—if not your rumored smiling face.
Repent and sacrifice: Build an altar, burn
the flip side of each healthy desire.
We're talking serious grace.

A childhood lost has wet the altar wood
further dampened by the somewhat death
of love, whose heaven's mirror held to life
reminds us that our souls are good.
Such sacrifice! The thought rips out your breath.
The Aztecs knew to use a sharp, sharp knife.

Homage to the Gecko Lizard

Dropped in my dream down a short stair
you didn't break but puddled egg-like and green.
I could no longer hold you by your nape
to prevent your biting me. Still, I care
that you are gone; more, I grieve having been
afraid of your bite. Let long black curtains drape

everywhere the household of my troubled art
whose distancing skin you tried to break
through. I now know it for a tangled skein
—and dark, my yet unspinnable yarn.

Would it be indulgent to throw a wake
for one's reptilian brain?

Through how many endless dream rooms had I
borne you like a suspect, angered foundling?
Still, I feel your fountain spirit linger,
beneficent critic with unblinking eye.
Come back. I'll steel myself against your sting
—and vow to proffer a tentative finger.

Looking Back

I ask the coroner: "Drew,
what am I doing here?
"Shut up, Ed," he says, "lie back,
I've had a hard day, too."
The lesson comes clear:
It's life abundant I lack.

Good God, now where are you
on the eve of no more dawn?
Under the rug, nothing but dust.
In the closet only clothes (none new).
Out in the yard, only the lawn
and one lone concrete statue, noseless, bust-

less, hooked up to the garden hose.
Do you dream of empty mirrors, too?
Darlings, we are in the throes.
Tell me something—no, reveal it—new
that won't hook into residual fear.
"Drew, this has been one hell of a year."

About the Author

Ed Zahniser was a founding editor of Some Of Us Press, a former poetry editor of *Wilderness* and *Artz and Kulchur*, and is poetry editor of the *Good News Paper*. His poetry includes four previous books, five chapbooks, a Pushcart Prize nomination, and recording for Grace Cavalieri's "The Poet and the Poem" series at the Library of Congress. He writes a column for *Fluent*, blogs for *Adirondack Almanack*, and prognosticates for *WV Observer*.

A Viet Nam-era veteran, Ed Zahniser edited newspapers here and in South Korea. As senior writer and editor of the National Park Service Publications Group, he was awarded the U.S. Department of the Interior Distinguished Service Medal. He lectures widely on wilderness preservation and federal public lands topics. Bill McKibben has described Ed Zahniser as "...a freelance theologian telling more truth than all of the TV preachers and all of the TV pitchmen put together."

CPSIA information can be obtained at www.ICGtesting.com
Printed in the USA
LVOW08s1558220316

480252LV00002B/261/P

9 780996 648448